IMAGES OF ENGLAND

# STRATFORD-UPON-AVON
## AND BEYOND

The visitors come and walk up and down
And they say to themselves what a lovely old town
They look at the theatre, the birthplace and river
The house, the gardens and hither and thither

They come from Europe, the States and Japan
All for the memory of only one man
They take out their cameras and cry in delight
Just look at those houses – they're all black and white

They hurry and scurry and rush to and fro
But we have a Stratford that they do not know
The Stratford that takes us down memory lane
To moonlight and roses and sunshine and rain

So when it is crowded and people complain
About parking and pushing – 'We won't come again'
We think of memories and what used to be
And good old Stratford seems nearer to me

*This book is dedicated to my youngest sister*
*Christine,*
*who died tragically, aged 29,*
*in the Sierra Nevada, Mountains California, USA,*
*in June 1974.*

IMAGES OF ENGLAND

# STRATFORD-UPON-AVON
# AND BEYOND

John D. Oldfield

TEMPUS

To the Electors of the Stratford-on-Avon Division
of Warwickshire.

GENTLEMEN,
If you do me the honour to elect me as your Representative I shall support the following programme :---

1. FREE TRADE and a CHEAP LOAF.

2. REFORM of the LAND-LAWS.

3. ALLOTMENTS and SMALL HOLDINGS at a Fair Price.

4. FREE EDUCATION in Voluntary and Board Schools.

5. FREE and REPRESENTATIVE System of COUNTY GOVERNMENT.

6. FAIR TAXATION.

7. REFORM of PROCEDURE in the HOUSE OF COMMONS.

8. REFORM of the HOUSE OF LORDS.

No other important questions will come before the next Parliament, and therefore if you approve of the above measures I ask you to vote for me.

Faithfully yours,
**WILLIAM COMPTON.**

*Compton Wynyates, Nov. 27th, 1885.*

Printed by G. Boyden, 29, High Street, Stratford-on-Avon, Published by S. Mawer, 13 Guild Street, Stratford-on-Avon.

A copy of an election poster from 1885. Our politicians are still making some of these promises today, over 110 years later!

First published 1996, reprinted 2005

Tempus Publishing Limited
The Mill, Brimscombe Port,
Stroud, Gloucestershire, GL5 2QG
www.tempus-publishing.com

British Library Cataloguing in Publication Data.
A catalogue record for this book is available from the British Library.

ISBN 0 7524 0685 X

Typesetting and origination by Tempus Publishing Limited.
Printed in Great Britain.

# Contents

Introduction                                              7

1.   The Theatre on the River                             9
2.   Up Sheep Street to Ely Street                        17
3.   Wood Street to Rother Street                         21
4.   Henley Street                                        33
5.   High Street to Holy Trinity                          41
6.   Pubs, Restaurants and Hotels                         61
7.   Bridge Street                                        69
8.   Transport                                            77
9.   Shottery                                             85
10.  From Little Acorns…                                  91
11.  Stratford Miscellany                                 97
12.  Out and About around Stratford                       103

Acknowledgements                                          128

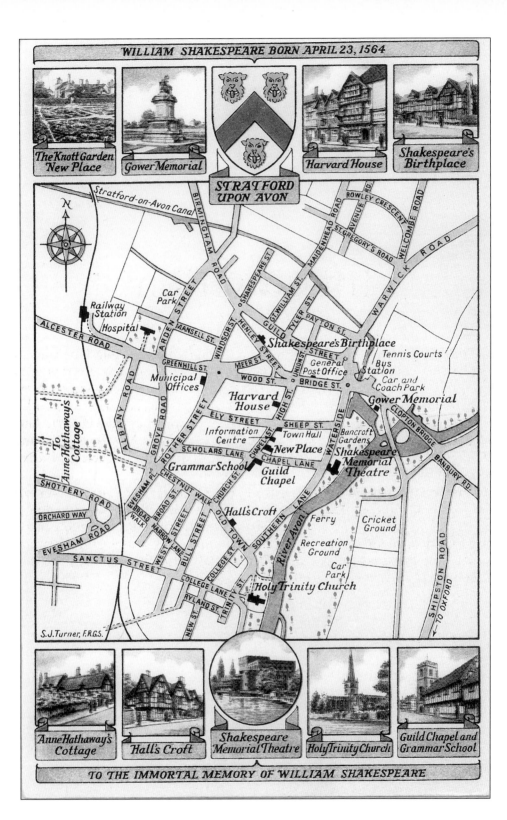

# WILLIAM SHAKESPEARE BORN APRIL 23, 1564

The Knott Garden New Place

Gower Memorial

STRATFORD UPON AVON

Harvard House

Shakespeare's Birthplace

Anne Hathaway's Cottage

Hall's Croft

Shakespeare Memorial Theatre

Holy Trinity Church

Guild Chapel and Grammar School

## TO THE IMMORTAL MEMORY OF WILLIAM SHAKESPEARE

# Introduction

When I accepted an invitation from the Chalford Publishing Company to compile this book I knew it would not be easy. My hobby is collecting old postcards and while I have a reasonably comprehensive collection of the Stratford upon Avon area, I was apprehensive about becoming an author because I am far from an expert on local history. My only previous claim to fame in the field of writing, was that I was educated at Belle Vue Boys' Grammar School in Bradford, West Yorkshire, which is where J.B. Priestley learned his trade.

Many books on Stratford have already been written and it is my intention that this book will complement rather than compete with any of them. I hope that my efforts will have proved worthwhile and that my selection of old photographs and postcards will evoke memories of this fascinating town, its people, its streets and its many fine buildings in this the year that Stratford celebrates its 800th anniversary. Happy reminiscing!

A magnificent display of produce at Robert Garrett's Central Auction Mart in Guild Street, 13 September 1907. This card was sent to one of Garrett's customers in Winchcombe and reads: 'Dear Sir, I have this day sent you to Toddington station 6 hampers for pheasants and shall be glad to have as many as you can send.' It was posted on 9 December, just in time for Christmas.

At about 8.30 p.m. on 8 May 1912 there was a disastrous explosion at the gas works, on Birmingham Road. The blast could be heard for miles around. Unfortunately, two men were killed and fifteen children left fatherless.

# One
# The Theatre on the River

*Occupying a commanding riverside site, the Theatre, set in its own gardens, can be seen at a distance from nearly every direction but particularly from a vantage-point across the river. The terraces overlooking the River Avon are a particularly attractive feature. The Theatre is a magnet that draws in people from all over the world to watch and appreciate the Shakespearean plays. Day-trippers in their hundreds come to this part of Stratford during the summer, not only for Shakespeare but for far simpler pleasures such as fresh air, the river and the wide-open spaces.*

The original Royal Shakespeare Memorial Theatre, built in 1876, and opened on 23 April 1879.

Destruction of the Memorial Theatre, 6 March 1926. The sign for The Black Swan public house can just be seen on the left. Photograph by Antona.

The Theatre well ablaze. Photograph by F.J. Spencer.

Crowds gather as firemen fight in vain to stop the flames. Photograph by Antona.

Left: inside the ruined Theatre. Photograph by Antona. Right: Lady MacBeth wringing her hands. Photograph by Raphael Tuck & Sons Ltd.

The modern Shakespeare Memorial Theatre, opened in 1932. Photograph by Antona.

A view of the New Theatre across Bancroft Gardens, with the Gower Monument and Shakespearean characters in the foreground – Lady Macbeth, Hamlet, Falstaff and Prince Hal.

The River Avon, *c.* 1906, with steam-boats for hire.

Waterside and the river looking towards the church, *c.* 1945.

The unveiling ceremony for the Stratford upon Avon Boat Club War Memorial, 21 May 1921. The Boat Club was founded in 1866 and although they had problems in their very early years they have prospered since the mid-1870s. Photograph by Antona.

Stratford upon Avon Regatta, 1908. Photograph by W.A. Smith.

The River Avon in flood at Clopton Bridge. The Avon regularly flooded until the River Authority introduced a weir and locks just downstream from the Theatre. The record height of a flood in Waterside is about 4 ft (1901) and about 3 ft in 1932 and Waterside is well above the normal river level.

Broken boats and debris with various interested onlookers at the tramway bridge.

Flooding on Waterside showing the premises of Warwickshire County Garage, *c.* 1932.

The river in more tranquil mood at Clopton Bridge. Photograph by Harvey Barton & Son Ltd, Bristol.

# Two

# Up Sheep Street
# to Ely Street

*This minor street leads up from the river to the town centre, but it was not until the end of the last century that business premises began to appear. Until then it had been purely residential. Today, one can find a host of different restaurants, antique shops and high-class clothes'-shops.*

The Town Hall, on the corner of Sheep Street and Chapel Street, c. 1910. The houses in the distance are in Ely Street. Photograph by W.A. Smith.

May Day celebrations in 1912 at the corner of Sheep Street and Waterside showing The Wheatsheaf public house.

Shrieves House, No 40 Sheep Street. This is one of the most important sixteenth-century buildings in the town. It was once occupied by corn merchants and cabinet-makers. Photograph by Walter Scott, Bradford.

The post office, Sheep Street, *c.* 1905. This was built in 1891 and was used until the middle 1960s, when it was moved to Bridge Street and then to its present home in Henley Street.

A group of tourists in Sheep Street, with the Bancroft Hotel in the background, 1930s. Photograph by Jerome Ltd.

Old houses in Ely Street. These were typical examples of the smaller types of dwelling common in Shakespeare's time.

# Three
# Wood Street
# to Rother Street

*Wood Street, the continuation of Bridge Street up through the town, comprises residential and shop premises and could perhaps be ranked third behind Bridge Street and High Street in terms of importance in Stratford. At the top of Wood Street we turn left towards Evesham to find Rother Street and the American Fountain. Here Stratford's weekly market is held each Friday on the site where a cattle market was held in former times. In the centre stands a memorial erected by George W. Childs of Philadelphia, known as the American Fountain. This was given to the town as a gift to celebrate Queen Victoria's Golden Jubilee in 1887. Overlooking the market area is The Old Thatch Tavern.*

Coronation Day celebrations (for King George V) in Wood Street, 1911, showing Barclays Bank on the right and Lacey's hardware store on the left.

Mayor's Treat parade, Wood Street. On the right is Eason's, gents' outfitters. Instead of the traditional Ball or Civic Dinner, the Major of Stratford gave the young people of the town a 'Treat'. This was a noisy party at a house out of town where large amounts of food were provided plus entertainment. Photograph by Bryan.

Pearce's Shakespeare Restaurant in Wood Street.

Armistice Day. The three buglers are B. Antrobus, M. Knowles and Sergeant Vallance. Note Boots the Chemist have taken over the corner premises from Lacey's (compare with p. 21).

Wood Street showing The Plymouth Arms on the left and The Horse and Jockey on the right. The American Fountain and The Old Thatch Tavern are visible in the distance.

J.J. Mitchell, baker and confectioner and producer of 'celebrated pork pies', No. 17 Wood Street, *c.* 1925.

Wood Street, showing Frank Organ, house furnisher, on the right, *c.* 1950.

Baum, family grocer and provision merchant, *c.* 1910. The shop is now Lacey's.

Schofield's, fruiterers and poulterers, with The Great Western Arms public house next door on the left. The National Westminster Bank now stands in the place of the inn. Photograph by Bryan & Smith.

Wimlett butcher's shop, by appointment to Her late Majesty The Queen (Victoria) and HRH The Prince of Wales, No. 7 Wood Street, *c.* 1910.

The Hippodrome roller skating rink, 26 December 1939. This was a large sports and social hall where all types of leisure pursuits were enjoyed.

Looking down Wood Street. The American Fountain in Rother Street is slightly obscured by the tourist bus going to Anne Hathaway's Cottage, *c.* 1925.

The Fountain Temperance Hotel behind (left) of the American Fountain, *c.* 1905. The White Swan Hotel can be seen on the right.

Ox-roasting outside The White Swan Hotel.

The Hampshire Regiment march from the railway station in 1915, Greenhill Street/Rother Street.

Old houses, Rother Street. The more modern building is the Congregational chapel and the fine medieval building to the left is Mason's Court. This is a superb specimen of early fifteenth-century domestic architecture.

Rother Street showing the premises of James Cox, baths and sanitary goods, *c.* 1910.

The nursing home and children's hospital, Rother Street. This building is now the Civic Hall.

The weekly Friday market in progress by the Fountain, *c.* 1960. Photograph by P. Inted.

An aerial view of Rother Street and the American Fountain, taken from an Airco machine flying above the town. Photograph by the Aircraft Manufacturing Co. Ltd.

# Four

# Henley Street

*Henley Street has seen many changes during its history, not least the problems encountered with modern-day traffic. Until quite recently, this was the main road out of Stratford town centre towards Birmingham. Because of the frequent traffic jams, the road system of Stratford was redesigned. Henley Street, today, is part-pedestrianised and part-one-way system.*

Henley Street, 1908. As we stroll along the street we can see Shakespeare's birthplace, an early sixteenth-century half-timbered property, the Public Library (opened in 1905) and the Shakespeare Centre which was opened in 1964 to commemorate the 400th anniversary of the poet's birth.

View along Henley Street, away from the town, during one of the celebrations. Photograph by Spencer, Stratford upon Avon.

This is the opposite view down Henley Street showing the birthplace of Shakespeare on the left and Barclays Bank in the far distance, *c.* 1910.

Henley Street at the turn of the century. Bryant's was Stratford's first sixpenny bazaar.

THE PUPPET CENTRE

LANCHESTER

39 HENLEY STREET
STRATFORD-UPON-AVON
WARWICKSHIRE

In complete contrast – the Puppet Centre which was at No. 39, Henley Street.

Sheep Street? No, this is an early artist's impression of Henley Street and the Birthplace.

May Day Festival celebrations, 1911. Here a team of oxen have halted outside Shakespeare's birthplace. Photograph by J. Jerome, Stratford.

The Stratford Arms public house. Next door at No. 40 is J.H. Cooper's fish and chip shop.

An unusual view of Henley Street at the corner of Windsor Street, featuring Guyver's Garage. Shakespeare Street can be seen in the distance.

Frank Organ, complete house furnisher at No. 61, Henley Street, *c.* 1910. Next door was Inglis' ladies' and gents' hairdresser, which was in those days the only hairdressers in the town.

Shakespeare's Birthday procession, 1912. Frank Organ's is again prominent.

A gathering at the Shakespeare Birthday Festival, 1930s. Photograph by Frank Packer, Chipping Norton.

Shakespeare Gift Shop at No. 41, Henley Street.

Looking into Henley Street with the Shakespeare Gallery Restaurant on the right. Note the road sign to Birmingham.

# Five

# High Street
## to Holy Trinity

*High Street, known locally as Up Street at the turn of the century, has many interesting and delightful old timbered buildings, of which the Garrick Inn and Harvard House are probably the most famous. The residential element has now been much reduced but until relatively recently High Street was where the leading lights of Stratford had their homes and shops. Next, we come to Chapel Street, where we can see, amongst other delights, Nash's House, The Falcon Hotel, the Town Hall and the Shakespeare Hotel. Then we arrive at Church Street, which leads into Old Town. We can see the former homes of Miss Marie Corelli at Mason's Croft and at No. 8 that of W.W. Quartermain, a well-known local artist whose work can be seen on many postcards (see page 55 for an example of W.W. Quartermain's work). Also here are the Guildhall, the Almshouses and Trinity College on the corner with Chestnut Walk. Then onwards into Old Town, by which name the area was already known in Shakespeare's days, along the street that leads us to the Holy Trinity church.*

Parade in High Street, with Hunter's on the right.

Hunter's, importers of provisions and tea-blenders, High Street showing a superbly dressed shop-front with hams and all manner of goods. This image was also used by the shop as a Christmas card, hence the 'Season's Greetings' in raised gold-coloured lettering on the right-hand side. The card probably cost a penny or two to produce. Nowadays, a postcard of this type would cost a collector around £30. Photograph by the Belgrave Electric Studio, Derby.

International Stores, High Street. The offices of the local paper, *The Stratford upon Avon Herald*, is next door.

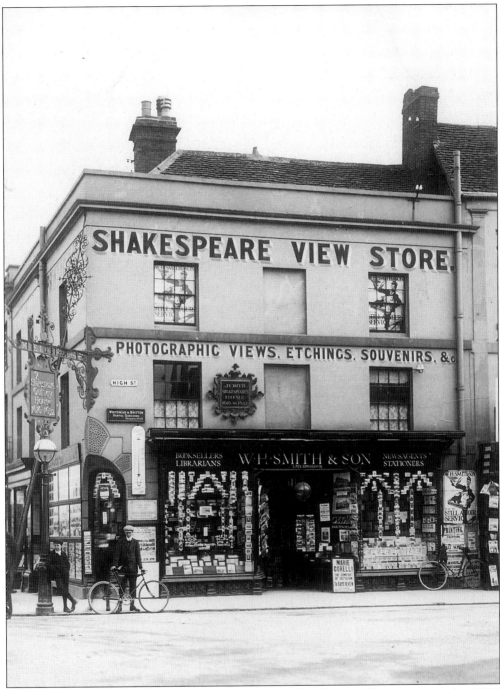

This was once the home of Shakespeare's daughter, Judith. The building was restored in 1923 by W.H. Smith & Son, who occupied the site from 1906 to 1922.

Fred Winter's shop at No. 31, High Street, *c.* 1920. The shop can be found in the new shopping precinct known as Town Square.

Tudor House in High Street, decorated for the 1907 Shakespearean Festival.

Celebrations in High Street. Note the photographer rushing along to get himself in position.

High Street, *c.* 1915. At Nos 10-11 was the local family firm of Morgans selling artist's colours and materials, plus stationery. The business was later sold to Midland Educational. Buckland, watchmakers and jewellers is next door.

High Street, *c.* 1910. A similar but earlier view of Morgans, this time with a three-wheeled motor-cycle prominent. Eccles' spectacle shop is next door.

The official opening in 1909 of Harvard House, High Street, by the United States ambassador and Miss Marie Corelli. This building is dated 1596 and is a fine example of Elizabethan timberwork, showing a great variety of carved ornamentation on its frontage. It is of particular interest to our American visitors as it was once the home of Katherine Rogers, mother of John Harvard, the founder of the American university. The property was bought by Edward Morris of Chicago who generously presented it to Harvard University in 1909.

The decorations are up for the Shakespearean Festival, High Street, 1908. Photograph by Bryan.

Shakespeare's Birthday celebrations, High Street, 1908. Ye Olde Garrick Inn is on the left.

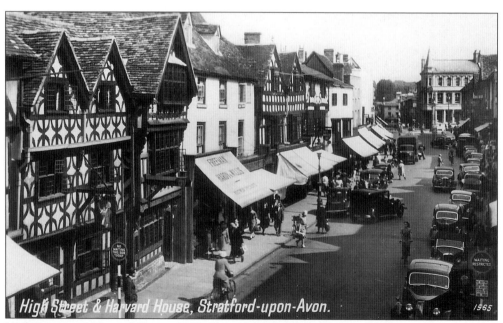

High Street and Harvard House, 1949. Photograph by Photo Precision Ltd, St Albans.

Chapel Street, 1907. The Gild (Guild) Chapel was founded in 1269. The Falcon Hotel is seen on the right.

The Town Hall, built in the classical tradition using Cotswold stone, at the corner of Chapel Street and Sheep Street. It was dedicated to the memory of Shakespeare in 1796 by the actor, David Garrick. During the Second World War it was used as a military hospital.

Two different perspectives of the Shakespeare Hotel and The Five Gables. The latter is one of Stratford's most famous hostelries and part of it dates back to early sixteenth century. In its early days it was called Bolton's Commercial, named after its proprietor. Photograph above by Harvey Barton & Son Ltd, Bristol. Photograph below by Kingsway Real Photo Series.

New Place Hotel, Chapel Street, *c.* 1910, showing a Riley advertising car on a promotional drive.

New Place, Chapel Street. This is the site of the house where Shakespeare lived in his retirement and where he died. Sadly, only the foundations of New Place remain today. The house shown in this photograph is Nash's House which is maintained by the Birthplace Trust. Thomas Nash married Shakespeare's grand daughter.

New Place Gardens and the Falcon Hotel. New Place with its ancient mulberry tree was bought by Shakespeare in 1597. The Falcon Hotel is a late fifteenth-century half-timbered building. It possessed the very first gas cooker in Stratford!

Shakespeare Festival procession, Church Street, 1910.

Outside the Almshouses, Church Street, *c.* 1910. One of the placards reads 'God bless King Edward'. The Almshouses date back to 1269. Photograph by Spencer, Stratford upon Avon.

Miss Marie Corelli's house in Church Street. Photograph by E.A. Schwerdtieger & Co., London.

At the beginning of the century, an almost legendary character, Miss Marie Corelli, moved into Stratford. She was a popular novelist, perhaps the Barbara Cartland of her time and a little risqué, but also a generous lady who gave large amounts of money to the town, provided, of course, that it was spent on her own ideas for improvements. She was closely involved with the Boat Club, perhaps because of her own nautical interest, which consisted of sailing a gondola on the River Avon. As one can imagine this caused a lot of excitement and interest in the early 1900s.

Marie Corelli enjoyed publicity, both good and bad, and was regularly at loggerheads with people in authority in Stratford. Her love of 'show-womanship' did not stop at the gondola. She was also driven around the town in a small carriage drawn by Shetland ponies, bells jingling, heralding her approach. Her splendid gondola, named *The Dream* arrived in Stratford in 1905, accompanied by a genuine Venetian gondolier. Unfortunately, he did not last for very long as he liked to spend the evenings drinking heavily in 'The Dirty Duck' public house. Following a drunken skirmish one night, during which he pulled a knife, he was dismissed and despatched back to Italy. Marie then persuaded one of her gardeners to act the part by dressing him up in a gondolier's outfit, so that she could continue her forays up and down the river.

Marie died in 1924, and the famous gondola fell into disrepair through lack of use and sadly sank in a lake. It was eventually raised and restored and is now still used in film and television work. A copy of the original can be seen on the river today due to the enterprise and skills of a local boatbuilder.

Miss Marie Corelli on the River Avon with her gondola, *The Dream*, and her Italian gondolier.

This postcard is by the local artist, W.W. Quartermain and again shows the gondola on the river, but this time the gardener is 'at the controls'.

Miss Corelli and her ponies galloping past the Guild chapel.

Giving the ponies a treat outside Halls Croft.

Left: Miss Marie Corelli with her dog. Right: presenting a cup at the Boat Club.

RIVER VIEW STRATFORD-ON-AVON MISS MARIE CORELLI'S GONDOLA.

The famous gondola on the river. Photograph by E.A. Schwerdtieger & Co., London.

Shakespeare's Birthday celebrations, Church Street. Trinity College is on the left, or as my old friends in Rome would say: 'Collegium Sanctae et Individuae Trinitatis AD MDCCCLXXII'! An imposing eighteenth-century building, it was a leading preparatory school for Woolwich and Sandhurst military colleges. In 1908, however, the whole college was moved to Maidenhead.

Church Street parade in 1913. Photograph by E. Anthony Tyler, Stratford upon Avon.

Typical town-houses in Old Town. Although the postcard is uncaptioned, this is probably a view of College Lane. Card by the Pimlico Publishing Co., London.

A wintry scene showing Avon Croft in Old Town.

SHAKESPEARES FESTIVAL PROCESSION 8 STRATFORD-ON-AVON 1910

Shakespeare Festival procession in 1910 through the gardens of Holy Trinity church.

Holy Trinity church, 18 July 1914.
Photograph by Judges Ltd, Hastings.

## Six

# Pubs, Restaurants and Hotels

*Apart from its Shakespearean fame, Stratford has always been well known for its many pubs, 'olde worlde' inns, hotels and restaurants. Nowadays there is a very cosmopolitan choice for those dining out ranging from Chinese, Indian, Greek, French and even one or two English eating-houses. The following chapter is a selection of pubs and 'eateries', past and present.*

The Unicorn Hotel, Bridgefoot. The proprietor at the time this photograph was taken was C.J. Huxley.

Ettington Park Hotel, just a few miles from Stratford. This top-class hotel was used by the Scotland football squad during Euro '96. Photograph by Antona.

Old King's Arms, Wood Street, c. 1905.

Plymouth Arms, Wood Street. Some readers will remember dancing here in the 1960s and 1970s.

The Shakespeare Gallery Restaurant at the corner of Henley Street and Union Street, now Barclays Bank.

The Cobweb tea-rooms, Sheep Street. This delightful eating-place is still very popular today.

The Red Horse Hotel in Bridge Street, *c.* 1939. Note the portico, taken from the Shakespeare Hotel. This is now a Marks & Spencer store.

The Swan's Nest Hotel, *c.* 1907.

Windmill Inn, Church Street, *c.* 1905. Photograph by E.J. Bryan.

The Red Lion, Warwick Road, *c.* 1905. Photograph by Bryan & Smith.

The Black Swan or as is it locally-known 'The Dirty Duck', Waterside, first licensed in 1792. Near to the Theatre, it is a natural drinking place for thespians and tourists alike.

Shakespeare Hostelrie, Chapel Street. Photograph by Antona.

The Old Thatch Tavern, on the corner of Rother Street and Greenhill Street. This is central Stratford's last thatched building, and has recently been re-thatched so that it continues for a few more years yet.

The William & Mary public house, Old Town. Photograph by Walter Scott, Bradford. This is now a fine public drinking house.

The White Swan Hotel, Rother Street. Photograph by Walker.

# Seven

# Bridge Street

*Bridge Street leads into the heart of the town from the Clopton Bridge. This wide thoroughfare originally had a line of buildings in the centre known as Middle Row but this was demolished in the nineteenth century. In Shakespeare's time all the main inns were congregated here. Whilst many of the present-day buildings have undergone elevational changes, the basic character of the street remains virtually unchanged. At the top of the street was once the Market House, built in 1821. This building was converted into Barclays Bank, as we know it today, in 1909.*

The last remnants of Middle row, Bridge Street.

On the corner of Bridge Street and Union Street, Valentine & Freeman are having a summer sale, *c.* 1910. Barclays Bank and a coffee shop now have this site, the National Westminster Bank previously having 'traded' here.

Procession of bicycles to celebrate the coronation of King George V in 1911. Photograph by Spencer, Stratford upon Avon.

Hoisting the King's flag, 1908. The George public house can be seen in the background.

The Red Horse and Golden Lion hotels, *c.* 1918, both old coaching inns. The site is now Marks & Spencer with the portico outside taken from the Shakespeare Hotel.

Crowds and decorations at the Shakespearean Festival in 1907. The Lloyds Bank building can be seen on the left-hand side. It had been rebuilt in 1867. Above the bank was the Judith Café.

Shakespearean celebrations, 1909.

Unfurling the flags in 1911.

The Mayor and his party at the celebrations in 1913.

War recruiting office, 1915. Photograph by Spencer, Stratford upon Avon.

Unveiling the War Memorial, 1922.

This is where the weekly Friday market took place. The cattle market was held at Bridgefoot at this time. Photograph by Judges.

Stratford's first female Mayor, Miss Annie Justins pictured during the 1929 Shakespeare's Birthday celebrations.

The illuminated Royal Crown, part of the town's celebrations of the coronation of Queen Elizabeth II in 1953. Barclays Bank can be seen behind.

# *Eight*
# Transport

*While, Stratford, long a bustling market town, does not have the depth or breadth of subject material one might expect from a larger town or city with trams and trolley-buses, it does have many things of interest to the transport historian. We can trace the history back to the old coaching days and right up to the present-day when we have fleets of buses on the streets, without a bus station in sight!*

Outside Shakespeare's birthplace. This photograph was taken en route from Manchester to London, quite a journey in those days. This is one of the private touring-cars belonging to Messrs J.M. Barrett & Sons of Pendleton, Lancashire.

Local photographer, J. Jerome, has captured a busy scene outside The Red Horse Hotel in Bridge Street. This coach and four was owned by local businessman, William Seymour Smith, the grandfather of our former Mayor, Mrs Pogmore. He owned in the region of twenty horses which were stabled behind The Plymouth Arms in Wood Street. In those days the stabling went right through from Wood Street to Ely Street. In addition to supplying Landau cabs for use in the tourist trade, his horses were used for local removals and for pulling Stratford's fire engine. The business was started at the beginning of this century and was continued by the family until the advent of motor transport.

An example of one of the early horse-drawn fire-fighting appliances.

The delivery vehicle of Walter C. Gibbs, baker and confectioner of No. 6 Wood Street, outside the house of Miss Marie Corelli.

Steam-driven delivery vehicle belonging to Flower & Sons brewery (registration number, AC 9), *c.* 1905. Note the tyreless wheels.

A bus in Stratford upon Avon railway station! This was a road railcar which ran through the streets of the town up to the Welcombe Hills.

Stratford upon Avon station approach, suitably decorated for the Shakespearean Festival. Photograph by Bryan.

Stratford railway station with a crowd of passengers on the platform, 1920s. In the 1960s, engines such as this were used for short local runs and were known affectionately as 'copper kettles'. Photograph by F. Moone's Railway Photographers, London.

A special train arriving at Stratford station. This train carried the US ambassador who was visiting the town for the opening of Harvard House in 1909. The train consisted of a Stratford upon Avon and Midland Junction railway engine (No 18, built by Beyer Peacock in 1908) with Great Central Railway coaches.

Stratford Blue was the well-loved and greatly missed bus company which operated in the town. Here, one of their double-deckers is parked outside The Mulberry Tree in Bridge Street.

A single-decker Stratford Blue bus.

What a service!

A more up-to-date Flowers Brewery vehicle, *c.* 1960. This is a Maudsley Mogul Mark II.

# Nine
# Shottery

*A small hamlet, just a few miles from Stratford town centre, Shottery is famous the world over because of Anne Hathaway's Cottage which is situated here. This was built in 1463 and has changed very little over the centuries. Despite a serious fire in 1969, when the cottage was the object of an arson attack, no sign of the damage can be seen today.*

Shottery, c. 1905, showing the Hathaway Temperance Hotel in the middle distance. Photograph by Bryan & Smith.

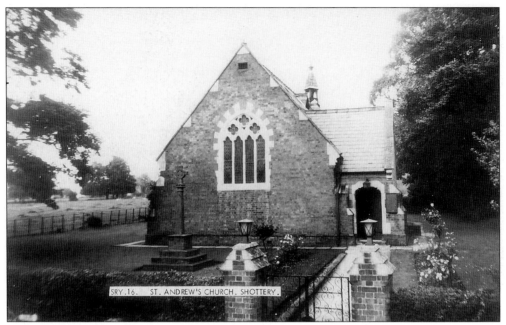

St Andrew's church, which was consecrated in 1870.

St Andrew's School. This building was originally a tithe barn in Redditch!

The centre of the village showing an old gentleman sweeping up.

The Tapestry Tea House where Devonshire teas cost the princely sum of one shilling.

The Silver Cock Tea Rooms, *c.* 1910. Photograph by W.A. Smith.

Re-thatching Anne Hathaways's Cottage.

Shottery Road, 1912. Photograph taken by J. Jerome, before any houses were built on the left-hand side of the road.

Anne Hathaways's Cottage, 1914. Photograph by Kingsway Real Photo Series.

# Ten

# From little acorns…

One of the business success stories in Stratford is the National Farmers Union Mutual Insurance Society Limited. The idea of an insurance company run by farmers for farmers was first mooted in 1910 in A.B. Smith & Sons' tea-shop in Chapel Street. Seven working farmers set up the company which was originally known as the Midland Farmers Mutual Insurance Society. Their first office was the farmhouse of one of the seven, James Black, at Clifford Chambers. In 1911, they moved to No. 9 Guild Street where they occupied just one room. In the first year a grand total of 70 policies were issued.

As business expanded, they had to move to slightly larger premises at No. 27 Bridge Street, where they stayed from 1916 to 1920 when continued success meant that yet larger offices were required. Fortunately, Maugersbury House in Church Street became available and the Mutual quickly purchased it and moved in. In 1925 they formed a subsidiary company – Farmers Commercial – which since 1931 has traded as that well-known company, Avon Insurance.

In view of the quantities of stationery that was being used by the growing society, it was decided that it would be beneficial to team up with a local firm of printers and so in 1930 they took on board Edward Fox. This partnership lasted for well over sixty years.

In 1984 the company made a major move to their brand-new flagship head office at Tiddington. The building, faced with pale Bath stone which shines almost white in sunlight, has been described by some as giving the impression of a sleek Cunard liner sailing in green pastures. An idea, sown by seven farmers in 1910, has now grown into a multi-million pound business, being the largest employer in the area, the benefits of which have been enormous to the town.

For almost a month last summer, as part of their preparations for Euro '96, the Scotland team stayed at a local hotel (see p. 62) and used the NFU Mutual's Sports and Social Club as their training base taking advantage of the excellent leisure facilities provided there. A TV centre was set up for the BBC and ITV, plus many other European companies, and broadcasts were regularly made from the club. With the Scotland squad and management being excellent ambassadors for their country, the whole event proved to be a major PR coup for the NFU Mutual. People came from miles around to watch the players train and have practice matches.

The original seven farmers:
J.W. Lowe, M. Burman, J. James,
C. Friend, J. Metters, J. Henson,
A.H. Pearce, plus J.R. Black, the
first secretary.

The office premises above the café at No. 27
Bridge Street.

The premises of Edward Fox in High Street.

Head office of the National Farmers Union Mutual Insurance Society in Church Street, 1924. The building is now occupied by Stratford-Upon-Avon District Council and is currently undergoing a multi-million pound renovation.

In 1932, this is how much you paid for a motor insurance premium.

Rear extension work in progress at the Church Street office. Notice how the frontage changed over the years.

An aerial view of Church Street and the surrounding area. Note, behind, the row of cottages which were utilised to build the branch office in Scholars Lane.

The new head office at Tiddington.

An aerial view of the new head office, 1984.

# *Eleven*
# Stratford
# Miscellany

*The photographs of this section have not fallen neatly into any of the previous chapters but presented together in the following pages they give a summarising flavour of the town over the years.*

The late, lamented Stratford picture-house in Greenhill Street which closed in the 1970s to make way for a new supermarket. Unfortunately, the supermarket moved on to more suitable premises after only a relatively short stay and the building is now occupied as offices. A new cinema is currently being built on the old Guyver's Garage site with an anticipated opening date in early 1997.

Maypole dancing at the Stratford upon Avon Shakespearean Festival, 1907.

Morris dancers at the Shakespearean Festival in 1907.

Miss Iris Courteney, the Rose Queen of Shakespeare Land, May 1939. She is now Mrs Iris Flynn, a proud mother, grandmother and, more recently, a very happy great grandmother.

A tranquil scene on the old tramway.

No book on Stratford would be complete without at least one photograph of the Mop. Here we can see Stratfordians enjoying themselves on T. Clarke's waltzer in 1912.

Stratford upon Avon Early Closers football team, 1905-06 season. The players and officials are from left to right, back row: R.J. Verney, W. Weatherhead, H.A. Wilkes, S. Symington, W. Eborall, A. Fisher. Middle row: A. Goucher, J.W. Harris (Deputy-Captain), W. Wall (Captain), G.H. Rose, F. Rodway. Front row: R. Hancox, R. Casswell, W. Drinkwater.

A fancy-dress day at Broad Street School, c. 1960.

A quiet part of Warwick Road. The only obstacle in those days was a 'pile' in the middle of the road, *c*. 1910. Photograph by W.A. Smith.

Catholic church, on the corner of Warwick Road, *c*. 1910. Photograph by W.A. Smith.

# Twelve

# Out and About around Stratford

*Within a few miles of Stratford upon Avon, a large number of interesting and picturesque small towns and villages can be found in the three counties of Warwickshire, Worcestershire and Gloucestershire (see map below). Some, like Stratford, have become crowded with tourists, while others still retain most of their original features and remain unspoilt to this day. Hopefully, readers will find something to interest them in the following pages. The villages have been arranged in alphabetical order to make the chapter more accessible.*

*We all have our own particular well-loved places for a variety of different reasons. Speaking from the heart, my favourite can be found on page 115. This is where I courted my wife when she was a young girl and where I was first introduced to proper country living!*

The forge, Alderminster. Photograph by Antona. Situated 4½ miles south-east of Stratford on the River Stour, there are two features in this village to attract the attention of motorists travelling south to Oxford. The first is a remarkable row of cottages built alike and widely spaced along the road and the second is the church with its massive central tower some 700 years old. The Norman style of architecture can be seen in the walls of the church and in the four arches of the tower.

Arrow Stores, grocer's and general cash stores. M. Dennis, the proprietor also advertised as a high-class pastry cook and confectioner. The village of Arrow is situated one mile south-west of Alcester on the river Arrow. Its cottages are along the busy main road to Alcester and at first glance there seems little to tempt the traveller to stop here. However, a closer look, reveals a lovely small church overhung by trees, with a tower, said to have been designed by Horace Walpole. A sculpture showing Sir George Seymour in his admiral's uniform is on view. The Seymour family lived in the great house in the park – Ragley Hall.

Church Lane, Aston Cantlow, 1914. A pretty village in the valley of the River Alne, 5½ miles north-west of Stratford, Aston Cantlow has a fine old street, traces of a moat and ancient earthworks, a few relics of a castle and an old guildhouse, now cottages. However, the village is more famous for the time when Mary Arden came from Wilmcote and John Shakespeare from Snitterfield for the union that was to give the world one of its greatest Englishmen. It is believed that they were married in this church among the trees overshadowing the small school.

The King's Head public house, Aston Cantlow. Photograph by Antona.

Bidford bridge. The bus was from the Leamington & Warwick Electrical Co. Ltd.

High Street, Bidford-on-Avon, $3\frac{1}{2}$ miles south of Alcester, 1909. The shop on the left is W. & A. Gilbey, wine and spirits seller. Next-door is a hairdressing salon with bicycles also for hire. The church of St Lawrence in Bidford has a thirteenth-century tower but the original church of the same date was remodelled in the last century. The bridge was first built in the fifteenth century. It replaced a ford across the river, which was used by the Romans and Charles I amongst others.

Bidford-on-Avon football team. The players and officials are, from left to right, back row: Chris Russell, Doug Partridge, Des Webb, Gerald Edgington, Louis Barry, Larry Dare, John Locke, Ian Lewis. Front row: Roger Busby, Graham Jackson, Reg ('Titch') Watson, Phil Nicholls, Nicholas Clarke.

The railway station at Binton, four miles west of Stratford. This village stands on a little wooded hill and looks across the valley of the Avon. It was one of the last English villages that knew Captain Scott before his ill-fated attempt to reach the South Pole. His brother-in-law, Lloyd Bruce was the vicar here.

The bridge over the River Avon at Binton marks the boundary with Welford-on-Avon. The public house is The Four Alls. The pub still has a sign reading, 'The King Rules For All, The Parson Prays For All, The Soldier Fights For All, The Yeoman Works For All'.

The post office, Binton. Photograph by Bryan & Smith, *c.* 1905.

BROOM VILLAGE.

A busy day in Broom village, three miles south of Alcester. This village is set amid a cornucopia of orchards and fields of soft fruits, cabbages, sprouts and cauliflowers. A mill on the River Arrow gives an air of added prosperity. Broom Court, with its Jacobean portal with Tuscan columns, and the fifteenth-century timber-framed Broom Hall are nearby. Photograph by E. Manley, Hay Mills Studio, Birmingham.

A superb scene outside Albert Tanner's in Chipping Campden, 9½ miles south-east of Evesham. Tanner was agent for GWR (Great Western Railway) Company goods and parcels and he also offered good stabling. Chipping Campden is one of the most charming villages in Gloucestershire and it has been said by a traveller that merely to walk down the long main street is a recipe for happiness. 'We look down on Campden from high roads and it is a joy to see this Cotswold village, houses built of Cotswold stone by Cotswold men with their canopied doorways, charming gables and oriel windows'.

The post office in Clifford Chambers, two miles south of Stratford, c. 1905. This village on the River Stour has a small but interesting church with a street bordered with grass and planted with trees leading to a seventeenth-century manor house. Some would have you believe that Shakespeare was actually born in the village because his mother lived here for a while when the plague came to Stratford.

Ebrington, c. 1939. Photograph by Wheeler. This village, two miles north-east of Chipping Campden, is known locally as Yubberton. So deep are the streets cut into the hillside here that everything in this fascinating village seems perched on a bank looking down from behind flower-decked walls and gardens. There are thatched roofs and yews trimmed like peacocks and also splendid views of the Cotswolds and the Vale of Evesham from the hills above. Hidcote Manor is near-by.

The post office in Ettington. The shop next door is offering Foster and Clark's 2d soups. Photograph by Antona. Ettington is $5\frac{1}{2}$ miles south-east of Stratford on the Banbury Road. A new church and an old tower stand at the crossroads.

Snitterfield Street in Hampton Lucy, four miles north-east of Stratford. Situated on the River Avon, this village has an impressive nineteenth-century church built by Thomas Rickman, who made his name as a pioneer in the Victorian Gothic revival. Photograph by E.J. Bryan.

Snitterfield Street, Hampton Lucy, *c.* 1910.

A typical thatched cottage in Harvington, $3\frac{1}{2}$ miles north-east of Evesham, 1938. This is an old village of much charm with black and white houses lining the road which winds up the hill to the church.

The post office in Ilmington in 1961. Note the adverts for Craven A cigarettes and Aspro! The vending machine is dispensing YZ chewing gum. Ilmington is a hillside village, off the beaten track, $3\frac{1}{2}$ miles north-west of Shipston on Stour, where the plains of Warwickshire rise up to the Cotswolds. It has a seventeenth-century gabled manor house and among the trees a Norman church with a battlemented tower.

Southam Street, Kineton, 1925. Photograph by Antona. A small market town, nine miles south-east of Stratford, Kineton is a settlement of great antiquity situated on the banks of the River Dene. About three miles away is Edgehill where the first battle of the Civil War took place in 1642. The streets of Kineton were then crowded with the horses and wagons of the Roundhead forces who were trying to intercept the King's march from Worcester to London.

Delivery men and boy at Long Compton, five miles south-east of Shipston on Stour. The church here dates from the thirteenth century but was altered drastically in the 1860s and first decade of the nineteenth century. The thatched lychgate at the entrance to the church of St Peter and St Paul is a cottage from *c.* 1600 with the lower storey removed. Photograph by Percy Simms of Chipping Norton.

The old Police House, Long Marston, $5\frac{1}{2}$ miles south-west of Stratford. This was the family home of my wife until we were married. This leafy-laned village has a group of charming old houses and cottages which are pictures of contentment in their lovely gardens. Charles I fled here after the Battle of Worcester and adopting the name of Will Jackson 'went to work' in the kitchen of a house which still stands today, known as King's Lodge.

The Grammar School, Long Marston, 1908. Photograph by W.A. Smith.

Mason's Arms public house, Long Marston, c. 1910. Photograph by W.A. Smith.

The post office, Mickleton, three miles north of Chipping Campden. Lying just below the Cotswolds, on the edge of Shakespeare country, Mickleton has some fine architecture in its Tudor and Queen Anne buildings. The church is set among luxuriant trees and is approached by an ancient stone path. Its tower is 600 years old and in the upper room the boys of poor families went to school from the middle of the seventeenth century until the nineteenth century. Photograph by Frank Packer, Chipping Norton.

Mickleton village street in 1908.

Friday Street, Pebworth, 1906. Photograph by Cymru. This village lies five miles north-west of Chipping Campden. Situated on the border of Gloucestershire and Warwickshire, it is the most easterly of Worcestershire villages. Two winding streets cross near the church and the houses are set in an informal way among trees. The church is medieval with a fifteenth-century tower. Outside the village, Pebworth manor house is Elizabethan, with traces of a moat, now dry.

Mason's Arms public house, Pebworth.

The Black Horse public house (proprietresses Annie and Sarah Harrison) in Watery Lane, Shipston on Stour, eleven miles south of Stratford. The inscription on the water trough reads: ' "A good man is merciful to all God's creatures." The gift of Richard Badger, 1902.' The flavour of other days is in all its streets where the houses and inns are from the Georgian period. Shipston has long been a market town and was formerly one of the busiest sheep markets in the country and at the heart of a flourishing local woollen industry. It is the most important settlement in the Feldon – the fertile and gently undulating area south of the River Avon. Photograph by Frank Packer, Chipping Norton.

Maypole dancers in High Street, outside the George Hotel, Shipston on Stour, May 1930. Photograph by Batt of Bourton.

119

May Day celebrations in Shipston, 1939. Amongst the crowd gathered outside the garage of Vin Davies in Church Street are: Mr & Mrs Pratley, Mr Saunders, Mr Begley, Mr Hartwell, Maggie Sutton. Arthur Adams, Stanley Mace, Fred Beale, Mrs Orchard, Bill Price, Ernie Freeman and Mr Jefferies.

Church Street, Shipston on Stour, showing the picture-house on the right. Good stabling is advertised as available at The Red Lion. Photograph by Antona.

Church Street, Shipston on Stour, with the Stour Garage and The Red Lion prominent on the left. Pettipher's Garage is on the right.

Pettipher's Garage in Church Street, Shipston on Stour, c. 1911. On the reverse of this postcard, Mr Eric Pettipher has written to a client: 'Dear Sir, ref. the cycle hired on May 15th. Will you please buy it for 25/-? The price for hiring comes to more than this as it will soon be 5 months.'

The church in Snitterfield, 1929. Situated 3½ miles north-east of Stratford, the village stands high in the Warwickshire countryside, with winding lanes, many good old houses and a fourteenth-century church. So high does the village stand that at the church door, the visitor is level with the top of the tower of St Mary's in Warwick. In the sixteenth century, Shakespeare's grandfather Richard lived here with his two sons, John and Henry. While Henry stayed in the village and died poor, John left for Stratford in 1551 and then married Mary Arden in Aston Cantlow, Thirteen years later their son, William was born. Perhaps a lucky '13' for Stratford. Had the farming been better or had John been a little less ambitious, then 'the Bard' might conceivably have been born in Snitterfield.

The post office in Snitterfield. Photograph by Antona.

Roasting the ox at Southam Mop in 1913. Situated nine miles south-east of Warwick, Southam is a small old market town traditionally associated with the Battle of Edgehill. The parish church of St James was built on high ground overlooking the valley of the River Itchen and it still stands on the edge of the town's market square, as it has done for the last 600 years. It has a large chancel, nave and aisles with a spire some 120 feet high. In years gone by, Southam was considered to be so important that it was allowed to make coins of the realm. Its mint is now a public house.

Meeting of the hunt, in front of the premises of Lewer, cycle agents and repairers, Southam, 1908.

High Street, Welford on Avon, looking towards The Bell Inn, 1923. Photograph by Antona. The village of Welford lies four miles south-west of Stratford, in a lovely setting on a peninsula formed by a loop in the River Avon. Much of the parish church of St Peter is Norman, although it was greatly restored in 1866. This is one of the few places which still preserves its maypole on the village green.

The Bell Inn (proprietor Levi Stanley) and E.G. Griffen, baker and confectioner, Welford on Avon. The latter building was the village shop and post office, now sadly closed.

Avondale House and Church Lane, Welford on Avon, 1906.

Erecting the new maypole in Welford on Avon, May 1927.

Chestnut Square, Wellesbourne, five miles east of Stratford. Photograph by Antona. In the late nineteenth century this village was the centre of a movement for improving the life of the agricultural labourer. Meetings were held in the evenings by the light of candles stuck in the bark of old trees. Such was the national interest that the London papers sent artists here to draw pictures of the happenings.

The church, Weston on Avon, 3½ miles south-west of Stratford. An interesting feature of the church is its grand array of north windows, all of which date from the fifteenth century. Weston is a thatched-cottage village by the River Avon and a lovely place to get away from the pressures of town and city life. John Trapp was the vicar here during Charles I's reign. He was also a master at Stratford Grammar School.

Wilmcote railway station, c. 1906. Situated three miles north-west of Stratford, Mary Arden once lived in a cottage in Wilmcote. This has stood here for five centuries and is one of the very best of the Shakespeare cottages. It has a huge fireplace, a monk's table from c. 1480 and herring-bone timbering in the roof of a wing added to the property some 400 years ago. People come from all over the world to pay homage.

The post and telegraph office, Wilmcote. Note the gas light outside and the well-dressed little girl sitting by the water pump in the background.

# Acknowledgements

The greater part of this collection of old photographs has come from the author's own collection, but many thanks are due to the following for their invaluable assistance in giving and lending old photographs, help and advice:

Dr Robert Bearman and the staff at the Shakespeare Birthplace Trust Archives; Bill Cooper and the NFU Mutual Archives Department; Larry and Elaine Dare; Mrs Iris Flynn; Guy Mascord; Monty, my trusty companion; William and Elisabeth Myers, historians of Saltash, Cornwall; Mrs Muriel Pogmore, former Mayor of Stratford; the two old retainers, Dorothy and Brenda Sandland, circa 1930s; Emily and Jack Stephens, Torpoint, Cornwall – inspirational!

Last but not least, thanks to my lovely wife, Pamela, for her wholehearted support.